Josephine and her Dishwashing Machine

Josephine Cochrane's Bright Invention Makes a Big Splash

written by
Kate Hannigan

illustrated by
Sarah Green

CALKINS CREEK

AN IMPRINT OF ASTRA BOOKS FOR YOUNG READERS

New York

"The woman of the future will have the memory of Josephine Garis Cochrane in grateful remembrance. It was she who invented the machine which has set woman free from the most slavish and disgusting task of housekeeping—dishwashing."
—The Daily Picayune, *April 2, 1892*

Josephine Garis Cochran was a modern woman who wasn't afraid to get her hands dirty.

She kept a modern house, wore modern gowns, even added an *e* to her last name—*Cochrane!*—to give it just the right modern touch.

Like many people rebuilding their lives in the years after the Civil War, Josephine looked ahead to a brighter future.

One night after a dinner party, Josephine noticed something that made her breath catch. Her cups were cracked! Her dishes dinged! Her chowder bowl chipped!

She marched into the kitchen, plunged her hands into the murky water, and tried to fix the problem.

She soon regretted that decision. Stuck at the sink washing dirty plates, Josephine's fingers weren't free to tickle the ivories at the piano.

Or pick her favorite flowers from the garden . . . or spread sweet frosting atop tasty cakes . . . or even scratch the furry ears of her beloved hounds!

There must be a better way!

In the 1870s and '80s, inventors were hard at work.

Margaret E. Knight built a machine to produce paper grocery bags.

Thomas Edison was tinkering with the electric light bulb.

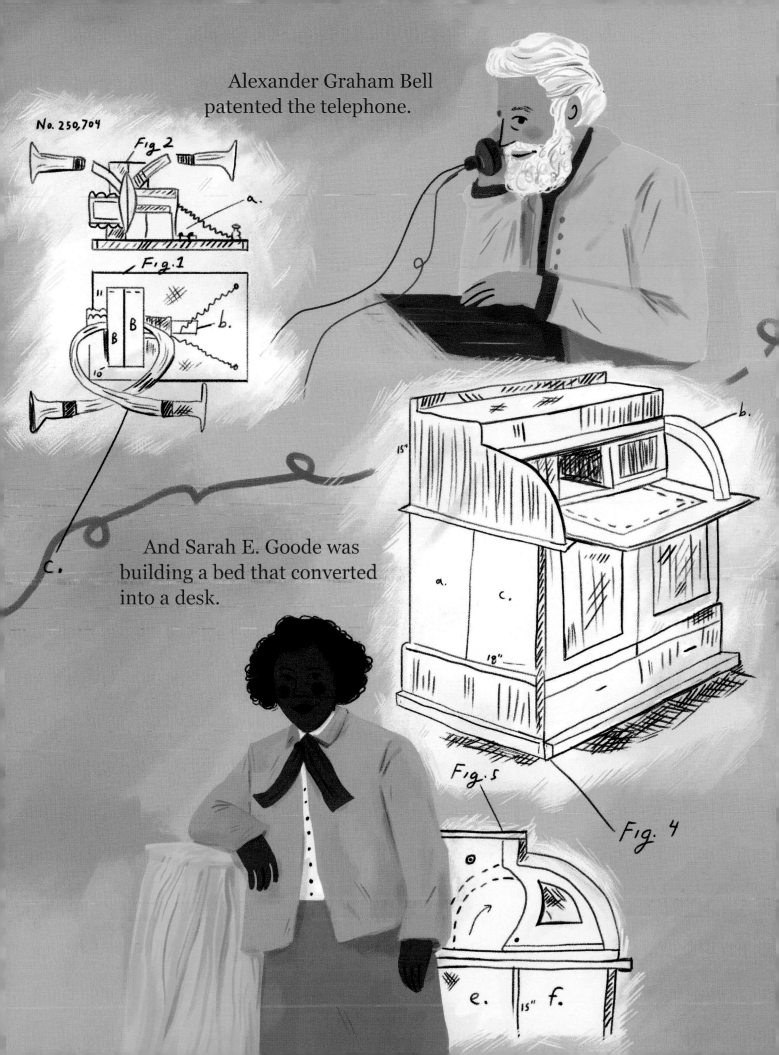

Alexander Graham Bell patented the telephone.

And Sarah E. Goode was building a bed that converted into a desk.

Josephine's blood also pumped with an inventive spirit. Her father, John Garis, had conquered raging rivers by building bridges. Her great-grandfather, John Fitch, had mastered water travel by designing steamboats.

She wanted to triumph over water, too.

Josephine pulled books off the shelves, determined to find a way to keep her precious dinnerware safe from dings and nicks.

She pondered.

She sketched.

She tinkered.

She studied a dishwashing invention built in 1850. But it just splashed water around without much cleaning.

There must be a better way!

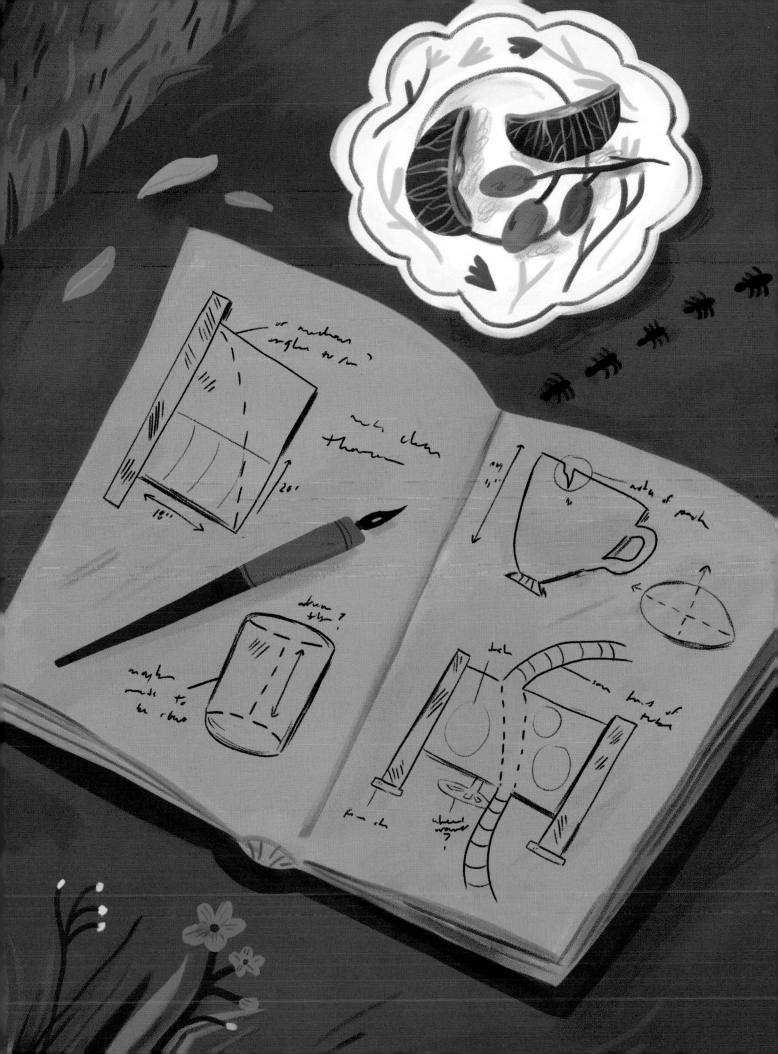

Josephine rolled up her sleeves.

She measured saucers and soup bowls, calculating how big her contraption should be.

She used pliers and wires, shaping metal baskets to hold plates, glasses, and spoons.

She designed a wheel to lie at the bottom, spraying hot, sudsy water from a copper boiler. And a hand crank to power it all.

Working in the backyard shed with a mechanic,
George Butters, Josephine brought her idea to life.
When it failed, she started over. When she
was close, she kept refining.
Revising, reworking, rethinking.
Finally, like a crystal-clean goblet, things
began looking brighter!

But tragedy struck in 1883: Josephine's husband died. Debts piled up like dirty dishes. How could Josephine afford her dream of being an inventor? She thought of throwing in the towel.

There must be a better way!

PAST DUE!

DUE

MPORT

Like drops of water trickling into a bucket,
Josephine paid her bills a little at a time.
     And she returned to the backyard shed to polish
her dishwasher design. Josephine and George tested
and tinkered and pushed and persevered until she
was satisfied.

Josephine had to act fast. If she didn't protect her idea, someone might steal it! She mailed her designs to the United States Patent Office, crossed her chapped fingers, and hoped for the best.

Days after Christmas the following year, Josephine received one of the best gifts of her life: Patent No. 355,139.

Few patent holders wore petticoats!

"My invention relates to an improvement in machines for washing dishes, in which a continuous stream of either soap-suds or clear hot water is supplied to a crate holding the racks or cages containing the dishes while the crate is rotated so as to bring the greater portion thereof under the action of the water."

—Josephine Cochrane, patent application, December 31, 1885

Josephine needed investors to build her dishwasher business. But no one could imagine a woman running a company. She would have to resign! After all the years she'd spent trying and failing and trying again, Josephine couldn't bear to step aside.

There must be a better way!

WORLD'S FAIR

Fig 3

Parts 3,4

Fig 5

fur

Fig. 4

gear

COLUMBIAN

Her invention was meant to spare dishes from chipping—and spare women from hours at the sink so they could do whatever they wanted. And what Josephine wanted was to build her business. "I cannot let go of the invention. I want to run the thing myself."

She read about a world's fair called the Columbian Exposition opening in Chicago in 1893. People from every continent were coming. Josephine decided to exhibit her machine, but would it stand out from the rest?

WORLD'S FAIR

Fig. 2

Fig. 1   Parts 1-6

EXPOSITION

Fig 8

Josephine's dishwasher took home the highest prize! It won for "best mechanical construction, durability and adaptation to its line of work."

Orders began pouring in from hotels, restaurants, and even schools and hospitals. The Garis-Cochrane Dish-Washing Machine Company soon outgrew the backyard shed.

By 1898, Josephine opened a bigger factory near Chicago. She filed for new patents—adding motorized power and reducing the number of pipes—and placed her reliable partner, George, in charge of factory operations.

People marveled at how her machines washed over a hundred dishes in minutes, and how the scalding-hot water killed germs better than handwashing. Josephine's company grew more successful every year, but sales into homes weren't catching on.

Josephine didn't worry. She updated her designs. She improved her factory's production. She knocked on more doors.

Even in her seventies—gray-haired but determined as ever—Josephine jumped on a train to New York. Marching into the city's modern department stores and soaring hotels, she kept on selling her invention to new restaurants there.

"Hope on, hope ever—that is my motto. It is a good world, and getting better every day . . ."

Eventually her dream of dishwashers humming in home kitchens came true. Instead of standing elbow-deep at the sink, women and men and even children had more time to do the things they loved—like playing the piano . . . picking flowers . . . frosting cakes . . . and scratching their beloved hounds' ears.

There was a better way.
And Josephine Cochrane found it!

*"Every woman is ingenious about her own house,
and I know many women who have invented clever things.
My next-door neighbor here, a few years ago,
invented a splendid contrivance for cooking eggs,
making coffee and browning toast
at the same time."*

Author's Note

Like any great inventor, Josephine Garis Cochrane (above) identified a problem and created something to solve it. But unlike most well-known inventors at the time, she was female. Born on March 8, 1839, Josephine came into a world that offered few rights or opportunities for women.

In this era, a married woman could not own property, sign legal documents, hold on to her earnings, or even get an education unless she had her husband's permission. Women inventors had to use their husband's names on patent applications, and they held little power to fight anyone who stole their ideas. Since Josephine was a widow, she had some amount of freedom to determine her destiny.

But she had to constantly battle mechanics who dismissed her because of her gender and businessmen who didn't want to work with a woman.

"You cannot imagine what it was like in those days . . . for a woman to cross a hotel lobby alone. I thought I should faint at every step, but I didn't—and I got an $800 order as my reward."

Always eager to improve her invention, she filed for multiple patents and kept building her business by securing more restaurant and hotel deals. But Josephine's 1912 trip to New York proved exhausting, and she died of a stroke the following year at age 74.

Josephine passed away in Chicago on August 3, 1913, when appliances like toasters and irons first began appearing in kitchens. As homes became wired for electricity, stoves, refrigerators, and washing machines became more common, too. Plumbing for hot-water tanks improved in the 1930s and '40s, and home dishwashers finally became more affordable.

Today, millions of dishwashers are installed each year, not just in restaurants, hotels, hospitals, and schools, but in home kitchens around the world. Just as Josephine dreamed.

"If I knew all I know today when I began to put the dishwasher on the market, I never would have had the courage to start,"

Josephine said looking back on her career. "But, then, I would have missed a very wonderful experience."

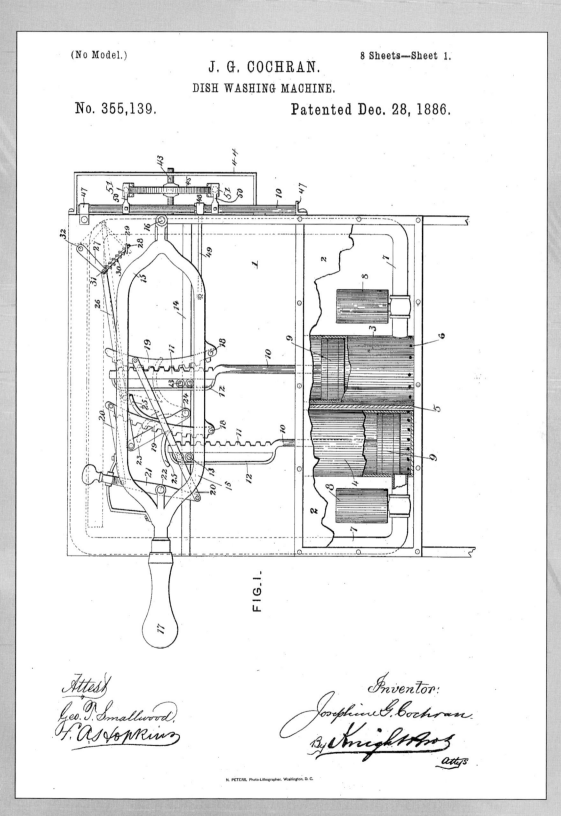

Notable Women Inventors

Mary Anderson received a patent for her car-window cleaning device in 1903. It was a swinging arm with a rubber blade, which the driver operated from inside the car by using a lever.

Georgia Bost, an ecologist, bred new types of hardy, fast-growing hibiscus flowers and received plant patents in the 1990s.

Yvonne Brill, a rocket scientist, patented her invention for propulsion systems for space satellites in 1972.

Marion O'Brien Donovan invented a diaper cover that was the precursor to the disposable diaper. In 1951, she received four patents for it.

Frances Gabe invented the self-cleaning house, patented in 1984.

Sarah E. Goode, a former enslaved person and the first African American woman to receive a U.S. patent, in 1885, invented a cabinet bed that could serve as a desk when folded.

Grace Murray Hopper figured out a way to "talk" to computers in the same language people used. Her 1956 invention of the first English-language compiler, called Flow-Matic, translated programming instructions into machine language.

Margaret E. Knight created many inventions, including a machine for making square-bottomed paper bags, patented in 1871.

Stephanie Kwolek invented Kevlar, a fiber used in bullet-resistant vests, and received a patent in 1971.

Hedy Lamarr, a film star and inventor, helped create a frequency-hopping secret communication system during World War II to keep enemies from intercepting classified information; the idea laid the groundwork for wireless communication like cell phones, Wi-Fi, and GPS.

Joy Mangano invented the Miracle Mop in 1990 and has patented over a hundred inventions.

Sybilla Masters, considered the first American woman inventor, received a patent in 1715 from England for a method of making cornmeal from maize. Though it was actually awarded to her husband, Thomas, it was described as an original invention "found out by Sybilla his wife."

Ellen Ochoa, the first Hispanic woman astronaut, patented three optics-related inventions she and her colleagues pioneered in the 1980s.

Elizabeth "Lizzie" J. Magie Phillips invented The Landlord's Game in 1903, which eventually became the board game Monopoly.

Rebecca Schroeder was only twelve in 1974 when she received the first of ten patents, for Glo-Sheet, a way to light up paper so she could do her homework in the dark.

Sarah Breedlove McWilliams Walker, later known as "Madam Walker," invented a hair treatment that became so popular in the early 1900s, she trained 25,000 women to sell her products, launched a beauty college, established a chain of beauty salons, and became the first African American woman millionaire.

Timeline of Fascinating Inventions

1791: August 26: John Fitch, great-grandfather of Josephine Cochrane, is granted a United States patent for the steamboat.

1818: Baron Karl de Drais de Sauerbrun invents the bicycle.

1824: Louis Braille invents the Braille system of reading for the blind.

1837: Samuel F. B. Morse invents the electric telegraph and, a year later, Morse code.

1876: Alexander Graham Bell invents the telephone, calling his assistant Thomas Watson with, "Mr. Watson, come here, I want to see you."

1880: Thomas Edison invents the first commercially practical light bulb.

1886: Josephine Cochrane invents the dishwashing machine.

1888: Theophilus von Kannel creates the revolving door.

1894: John Harvey Kellogg invents breakfast cereal flakes.

1896: Guglielmo Marconi invents the radio.

1902: Rose Michtom and her husband, Morris, create the teddy bear, and sell it in their shop.

1903: Wilbur and Orville Wright create the first engine-powered airplane.

1913: Mary Phelps Jacob invents the brassiere or "bra," freeing women from corsets.

1923: Garrett Morgan patents the traffic light.

1932: Ole Kirk Kristiansen invents Lego blocks.

1943: Jacques Cousteau and Emile Gagnan invent the Aqua-Lung, a scuba (self-contained underwater breathing apparatus) device.

1945: Percy L. Spencer invents the microwave oven.

1946: John William Mauchly and J. Presper Eckert introduce the Electronic Numerical Integrator and Computer (ENIAC), considered the first general-purpose electronic digital computer.

Sources

All quotations used in the book can be found in the following sources marked with an asterisk (*).

Books

The Book of Inventions by Ian Harrison (National Geographic Society, 2004).

Encyclopedia of Modern Everyday Inventions by David J. Cole, Eve Browning, and
Fred E. H. Schroeder (Greenwood Press, 2003).

Women Invent! Two Centuries of Discoveries That Have Shaped Our World by Susan Casey
(Chicago Review Press, 1997).

Newspapers and Magazines

American Heritage's Invention & Technology magazine, fall 1999, volume 15, issue 2.

Boston Weekly Globe, March 29, 1892.

*Chicago Record-Herald, November 24, 1912.

*Daily Picayune [New Orleans, LA], April 2, 1892.

Idaho Avalanche [Silver City, ID], March 17, 1894.

Milwaukee Journal [Milwaukee, WI], June 3, 1897.

New York Sun, April 9, 1892.

Websites

Digital Research Library of the Illinois History Journal: drloihjournal.blogspot.com/2017/01/
josephine-garis-cochrane-cochran-1839.html

*Google Patents: patents.google.com/patent/US355139A/en

National Inventors Hall of Fame: invent.org/inductees/josephine-garis-cochran

Wisconsin Historical Society: wisconsinhistory.org/Records/Article/CS2619

Websites active at time of publication

Acknowledgments

Grateful thanks to history lover Bianca Barcenas, a metadata specialist at the Chicago
History Museum; and to STEM expert, history lover, and mother of invention Gillian
King-Cargile. Thanks also to Chicago Public Library superstars Nate Parker and
Betsy Vera for their help with archived newspapers.

For the ever clever Katie Lang Musick —*KH*

To my nephew Henry, who loves dirty dishes —*SG*

Picture Credits

Alamy: 34; United States Patent and Trademark Office, Patent No. 355139A: 35; Computer History Museum: 36; Wikimedia Commons: 37 (top); NASA: 37 (middle); Smithsonian National Museum of African American History and Culture, Gift of A'Lelia Bundles / Madam Walker Family Archives: 37 (bottom).

Calkins Creek
An imprint of Astra Books for Young Readers,
a division of Astra Publishing House
astrapublishinghouse.com
Printed in China

ISBN: 978-1-63592-621-7 (hc)
ISBN: 978-1-6626-8014-4 (eBook)
Library of Congress Control Number: 2021925698

First edition

10 9 8 7 6 5 4 3 2 1

Design by Barbara Grzeslo
The text is set in Georgia.
The illustrations are done digitally.